ZOO ANIMALS
IN THE WILD

PENGUIN

JINNY JOHNSON
ILLUSTRATED BY MICHAEL WOODS

W

FRANKLIN WATTS
LONDON • SYDNEY

An Appleseed Editions book

First published in 2005 by Franklin Watts
96 Leonard Street, London EC2A 4XD

Franklin Watts Australia
Level 17/207 Kent Street, Sydney, NSW 2000

© 2005 Appleseed Editions

Created by Appleseed Editions Ltd,
Well House, Friars Hill, Guestling, East Sussex TN35 4ET

Designed by Helen James
Illustrated by Michael Woods

ISBN 0 7496 5977 7

A CIP catalogue for this book is available from the British Library

Photographs by Robert E. Barber, Corbis (Theo Allofs, Tom Brakefield, John Conrad,
Tim Davis, DESPOTOVIC DUSKO / CORBIS SYGMA, Firefly Productions,
Peter Johnson, Wolfgang Kaehler, Galen Rowell, Kevin Schafer, Paul A. Souders, Roger Tidman)

Printed and bound in Thailand

Contents

Penguins

When people first saw penguins they called them feathered fish. Penguins are birds, of course, not fish. But they swim so well that it's easy to get confused!

Penguins have feathers, but they can't fly. Their wings are shaped like flippers, and they use them for swimming. Penguins are some of the best swimmers of all birds.

There are 17 different kinds of penguins. Some kinds live in Antarctica, one of the coldest places in the world. But penguins live in warmer places, such as South Africa, too.

African penguins are the easiest to keep in a zoo, because they don't mind warm weather. In the zoo, African penguins have homes with cool salt water pools. Some of the pools even have wave machines and seaweed!

Some penguins have bright markings. The macaroni penguin has a tuft of orange and yellow feathers on its head.

The emperor penguin is the largest of all the penguins. It's about one metre tall – as tall as most three- or four-year-old children.

The little penguin is the smallest type of penguin.

Shaped for swimming

A penguin's body is like a torpedo – plump and rounded in the middle and pointed at each end. It is just the right shape for zooming through the water.

A king penguin
dives deep
as it hunts
for fish to eat.

A penguin has a short, stiff tail. It sometimes uses its tail to help prop itself up on land.

Most penguins have black, blue or grey feathers on their backs and white tummies. The feathers are very tightly packed together to keep water out when the birds swim. Penguins look very plump, because they have a thick layer of fat under their feathers to help keep them warm in cold water.

A group of emperor penguins marches to sea.

Life on land

A penguin has very short, stumpy legs.
It looks as though it doesn't have knees –
it does, but they're inside its body. A penguin's
feet are webbed, which helps it move in water,
and it has three sharp claws on each foot.

On land, penguins stand upright, using their claws to grip the slippery ice and snow. When they walk, they waddle along, swaying slightly from side to side

A penguin's flippers help it balance as it walks slowly across the snow.

and holding out their flippers. Most penguins can hop and jump too. Sometimes they find it quicker to lie down and slide over the ice and snow. They use their feet to push themselves along and as brakes to stop.

Sliding over the ice can be easier than walking!

Zoo penguins need plenty of rocks and walkways to play on and dive from.

Deep divers

Penguins are much more at home in the water than on land. They spend about three-quarters of their time in water, and they are fast swimmers.

Penguins can't fly in the air, but they look as though they are flying through the water as they flap their flippers. They twist and turn with amazing speed, using their feet and tails to help them change direction.

Penguins can dive deep too. They dive to catch fish, squid and other sea creatures to eat. Penguins can stay underwater for 15 minutes or more at a time.

When a penguin is swimming slowly, it pops its head up to the surface and takes a breath.

Zoo penguins need a large pool of water where they can swim and dive.

This is much longer than people can. Even though they are such good swimmers, penguins must still come to the surface of the water to breathe.

When a penguin is swimming fast, it leaps out of the water to breathe and dives back in again. This is called porpoising – porpoises do it too!

Living together

When penguins are on land, they gather in big groups called colonies. There may be thousands of birds in these noisy places. The penguins squawk and squabble to keep their own little piece of land for themselves.

A penguin colony is called a rookery. All these penguins together make a lot of noise.

Zoos usually keep many penguins together because they are happiest in big groups. There may be several different kinds of penguins living together.

Other seabirds sometimes steal and eat penguin eggs and chicks.

Penguins gather together when it's time to lay their eggs. Being in a crowd helps them keep their eggs and chicks safe from enemies such as large seabirds called skuas. Many penguins go back to the same nesting place and meet the same mate year after year.

Nesting

Most penguins don't make proper nests.
King penguins and emperor penguins
keep their eggs warm on their feet.

Other penguins lay their eggs in little hollows they scrape out of the ground. Some add grass and twigs or a few stones if they can find them. Gentoo and Adelie penguins like to make a ring of stones around their nesting area.

A nesting African penguin peeps out of its burrow.

The yellow-eyed penguin of New Zealand lays its eggs in a forest. It finds a dark tree hollow or another hole where its eggs will be safe.

Zoos give penguins special nesting boxes so they can hide with their eggs. The birds can add twigs or stones from their enclosure if they want.

A gentoo penguin perches on its rocky nest.

African penguins and little penguins nest in burrows or among rocks.

A yellow-eyed penguin by its tree-hollow nest.

Laying eggs

Penguins lay one or two eggs at a time. The mother and father birds usually share the work of keeping the eggs warm until they hatch. A penguin, like many other birds, keeps its eggs warm with its body.

When a baby penguin is ready to hatch, it calls to its parents from inside the egg. It chips its way out of the egg with a spike on its beak. This is called an egg tooth.

A king penguin keeps its egg warm with the big roll of skin on its tummy.

16

A gentoo penguin chick hatches from its egg.

At first, the chick has only a thin covering of feathers. Its parents have to keep it warm until it grows a thicker coat of soft, downy feathers.

Two chinstrap chicks snuggle up close to their mother.

Baby penguins

When a baby penguin is a few weeks old, its parents can leave it for a little while every day while they go to the sea to feed. They need to catch food for their hungry youngster too.

While they're gone, their baby stays with the other young penguins in a kind of nursery. The chicks huddle together to keep warm and stay safe.

When the parents come back, they feed their chick with food they regurgitate (bring up) from their own stomachs. When a chick has grown its first coat of adult feathers, it is ready to go into the water. It can swim straight away – it doesn't need any lessons.

Penguin parents in the zoo don't have to worry about catching food for their young. It's brought to them, so parenting is much less work than in the wild.

A young king penguin looks as though it's wearing a winter coat that's too big.

A penguin chick makes lots of squeaking calls as it begs for food from its mother.

Young penguins may be a bit scared the first time they jump into the sea. No one wants to go first.

Emperor penguins

The emperor penguin is the biggest of all the penguins. Emperors lay their eggs and bring up their young in the coldest place on Earth – Antarctica.

As soon as the mother emperor penguin has laid her egg, her mate rolls it on to his feet with his beak. The egg is kept snug and warm on his feet, covered by a big roll of skin on his tummy. The mother goes back to the sea, but the father stands there, caring for the egg for nine weeks in the bitter cold.

Soon after the egg hatches, his mate comes back. She keeps the chick warm while the father goes to the sea to feed.

Mother and father emperor penguins take turns looking after their chick.

Then the parents take turns to look after the chick and find food until the chick is big enough to find food for itself.

Emperor penguin chicks huddle together to keep warm while their parents find food. They take turns to stand in the middle of the group – the warmest spot.

A few zoos keep emperor penguins, but they need specially refrigerated homes. These homes are cold, but the birds don't mind if they're not quite as cold as Antarctica.

Feeding time

Penguins find all their food in the sea. They eat mostly small fish, squid and little shrimp-like creatures called krill. Penguins that eat fish usually have longer, thinner beaks than those that eat mainly krill.

Penguins are excellent underwater hunters.

Zoo penguins are fed fish such as small herrings and mackerel. Zookeepers often throw the fish into the water so the penguins have to dive and catch them. Zoo penguins have some extras, too, such as vitamins to help keep them healthy.

Inside a penguin's mouth there are many little spines that help it hold on to and swallow slippery, wriggling prey. Penguins chase their prey underwater and swallow it in one gulp. They don't come to the surface to eat.

Keeping clean

A penguin's feathers keep it warm and dry, so it takes care of them. When a penguin comes out of the water, it cleans its feathers. It uses its beak like a comb to remove any bits of dirt and to smooth any ruffled feathers.

Penguins make a type of oil in a place called a gland near the tail. A penguin rubs its beak in this oil and spreads it over its feathers. This helps to keep them waterproof. Cleaning and oiling the feathers is called preening.

Penguins spend up to three hours a day preening.

Even with all this care, a penguin's feathers still get damaged and worn out. Once a year, a penguin grows new feathers, and the old ones fall out. This is called moulting and it takes two to four weeks.

A penguin's feathers fall out in clumps when it moults. It doesn't look its usual smart self at this time.

Sometimes penguins preen each other's feathers. It helps to have someone to reach the awkward spots!

Eyes and ears

Penguins have big eyes, and they can see well under water and on land. Being able to open their eyes underwater is important when they're fishing.

Penguins are experts at tracking their prey underwater.

Penguins have very good hearing. A penguin can find its own partner or chick among thousands of other penguins just by listening for its call. The calls might all sound the same to a human, but to a penguin, each one is different.

When you look at a penguin, you can't see any ears, but it has two little holes, one on each side of its head. They are covered with feathers.

Just back from finding food, a penguin parent calls to its chick.

Penguin fact file

Here is some more information about penguins.
Your mum or dad might like to read this, or
you could read these pages together.

A penguin is a bird. There are 17 different species, or kinds,
of penguins. All penguins feed on fish.

Where penguins live

All penguins live in the southern half of
the world. There are no penguins at the
North Pole, so there's never any danger
of one being eaten by a polar bear!
Penguins spend most of their lives in the
sea but come to land to lay their eggs
and look after their chicks. This is where
different kinds of penguins breed:

Adelie penguin: Antarctica
African penguin: southern Africa
Chinstrap penguin: Antarctica and
    islands around Antarctica
Emperor penguin: Antarctica
Erect-crested penguin: islands
    around New Zealand

Fiordland penguin: New Zealand
Galapagos penguin: Galapagos Islands
Gentoo penguin: Antarctica and islands
Humboldt penguin: Peru and Chile
King penguin: islands around Antarctica
Little (or blue) penguin: Australia,
    New Zealand
Macaroni penguin: Antarctic islands
Magellanic penguin: southern South
    America, Falkland Islands
Rockhopper penguin: Antarctic islands
Royal penguin: Macquarie Island,
    Australia
Snares penguin: Snares Island,
    New Zealand
Yellow-eyed penguin: New Zealand

Penguin numbers

There are lots of most kinds of penguins, but a few kinds are now rare.
These include the erect-crested penguin, fiordland penguin, yellow-eyed
penguin, snares penguin, and Galapagos penguin.

Size

The emperor is the biggest. It is about 1 metre tall, weighs 30–38 kg,
and has flippers 30–40 cm long. The little (or blue) penguin is the smallest.
It is 40–45 cm tall, weighs only about 1 kg, and has 11–14 cm long flippers.

Find out more

If you want to know more about penguins, check out these websites.

Kelly Tarlton's Antarctic Encounter & Underwater World
http://www.kellytarltons.co.nz/home/page.aspx

KidZone: Penguins
http://www.kidzone.ws/animals/penguins

Seaworld: Penguins
www.seaworld.org/infobooks/Penguins/home.html

New Zealand Penguins
http://www.penguin.net.nz

National Geographic.com Kids: Penguins
http://www.nationalgeographic.com/kids/creature_feature/0101/penguins.html

Words to remember

Antarctica
The area around the
South Pole, where it
is very cold all year.

colony
A big group of animals
gathered together in one place.

downy
Describes a young bird's first soft feathers.
It loses these when it grows adult feathers.

flippers
Flippers are shaped like paddles. They are actually
the penguin's arms — it has flippers instead of wings.

gland
Part of the body that makes a special substance, such
as the oil penguins use when cleaning their feathers.

krill
Small sea creatures that penguins eat.

mate
Male and female penguins pair up to lay eggs and care for young. A penguin's partner is called its mate.

squid
A squid is a kind of shellfish. It has a long body, four pairs of long arms and two tentacles.

webbed feet
Webbed feet have flaps of skin between the toes. This makes the feet into little paddles to help the penguin move in water.

Index